How to Make Eggnog Like A Pro

Pro

The Finest Eggnog Recipes Assembled

BY: Alicia T. White

License Note!

I know you've read this and seen this in many other books and movies. Still, there's a reason why authors and filmmakers are so adamant about protecting their copyrights despite it being so annoying for you to see yet again… The thing is, lots of people infringe on copyrights, and this greatly affects our work negatively.

Thus, here we go again just so things are clear:

Do not make any print or electronic reproductions, sell, re-publish, or distribute this book in parts or as a whole unless you have express written consent from me or my team.

I spent over 4 months working on this cookbook, so I protect it like it's my baby! I know you can understand the value of working hard on something and wanting to protect your end product, so please help me by not infringing on the copyright or letting others do so.

Thanks!

Table of Contents

Introduction

Many households across the globe consume gallons of eggnog at their annual Thanksgiving and Christmas celebrations. There isn't a single recipe for eggnog that doesn't have its own special touch, and every family's version has its own distinct flavor. No one knows for sure where the tradition of drinking eggnog began. According to legend, English monks brewed the first batches of this beverage during a meditative session in the 14th century. The beverage has since become one of the most common alcoholic offerings throughout the winter season in the United States.

You may now enjoy this beverage in the privacy of your own home with the guidance of this book, *"How to Make Eggnog Like a Pro."* You will not only find out how to create traditional eggnog but also how to use it in a wide range of other recipes. There is not a single one of these dishes that won't leave a lasting impression on anybody who tries it this holiday season.

In any case, let's not dally any longer.

What are we waiting for?

OOOOOOOOOOOOOOOOOOOOOOOOOOOOOOOOOOOOOOOOOO

1. Homemade Eggnog

Yield: 3 to 4 Servings

Cooking Time: 20 Minutes

Ingredient List:

- 6 egg yolks, large
- ½ cup of granulated sugar
- 1 cup of heavy cream
- 2 cups of milk, whole
- 1 ½ teaspoons of nutmeg, grated
- A dash of salt
- ¼ teaspoons of pure vanilla
- ⅛ teaspoons of rum extract, optional

OOOOOOOOOOOOOOOOOOOOOOOOOOOOOOOOOOOOOOOO

How to Cook:

A. Add the large egg yolks and granulated sugar to a medium bowl. Whisk until creamy in consistency.

B. Place a medium saucepan over medium heat. Add in the heavy cream, whole milk, ground nutmeg, and a dash of salt. Stir well to mix and bring this mixture to a simmer.

C. Add half a cup of the milk mixture to the egg mixture. Stir well to mix. Then add in the remaining milk mixture and stir well until mixed.

D. Pour the egg mixture back into the saucepan. Stir well and cook for 2 minutes, or until cooked through.

E. Remove from the heat and add in the pure vanilla and rum. Stir well.

F. Pour the eggnog into a bowl and cover. Place in the fridge to chill for 1 hour. Serve after this time.

2. New York Eggnog Crumb Cake

Yield: 8 Servings

Cooking Time: 45 Minutes

Ingredient List:

- ½ cup of unsalted butter
- 1 cup of granulated sugar
- 2 eggs, large
- 1 cup of eggnog
- 1 cup of sour cream
- ½ teaspoons of vanilla bean paste
- ¼ to ¾ teaspoons of nutmeg
- 2 ½ cups of cake flour
- 2 teaspoons of baker's style baking powder
- ½ teaspoons of baker's style baking soda
- A dash of salt

Ingredient List for the icing:

- 3 tablespoons of eggnog
- 3 tablespoons of spiced rum
- 2 tablespoons of melted butter
- 1 ½ cups of powdered sugar

Ingredient List for the crumb topping:

- ⅓ cup of granulated sugar
- ⅓ cup of brown sugar, light and packed
- ¼ teaspoons of salt
- ¾ teaspoons of cinnamon
- 8 tablespoons of unsalted butter

- 1 ¾ cups of cake flour

OOOOOOOOOOOOOOOOOOOOOOOOOOOOOOOOOOOOOOOOO

How to Cook:

A. First, prepare the crumb cake topping. To do this add the granulated and powdered sugar, dash of salt, and ground cinnamon to a medium bowl. Stir well until mixed.

B. Add the melted butter and cake flour. Stir again until just mixed. Set this mixture aside.

C. Next preheat the oven to 325°F. While the oven is heating up, grease 4 miniature loaf pans.

D. Add the butter and granulated sugar to the large bowl of a stand mixer. Beat for 3 minutes or until fluffy in consistency.

E. Add the eggnog, sour cream, vanilla pasta, and large eggs to a separate bowl. Whisk until evenly mixed.

F. In another large bowl mix the cake flour, ground nutmeg, baking powder and soda, and a dash of salt. Stir well to mix. Add in the wet ingredients and stir again until just mixed.

G. Using an ice cream scoop, scoop three scoops into each greased pan. Top off with the crumb topping.

H. Place into the oven to bake for 30 to 35 minutes or until baked through. Remove and transfer to a wire rack to cool completely.

I. Then make the glaze. To do this use a medium bowl to mix the eggnog, rum, butter, and powdered sugar. Whisk until smooth in consistency.

J. Pour the glaze over the cakes. Allow it to sit for 5 minutes to set before serving.

3. Eggnog Muffins with a Cinnamon and Rum Spiced Glaze

Yield: 8 Servings

Cooking Time: 20 Minutes

Ingredient List:

- 1 ½ cups of all-purpose flour
- ½ cup of granulated sugar
- ½ tablespoons of baking powder
- ½ teaspoons of baking soda
- cup of eggnog
- 1 egg, large
- ½ stick of butter, melted and cooled
- 1 cup of powdered sugar
- 2 tablespoons of rum
- 2 tablespoons of eggnog
- ½ teaspoons of cinnamon

OOOOOOOOOOOOOOOOOOOOOOOOOOOOOOOOOOOOOOOO

How to Cook:

A. Preheat the oven to 375°F. While the oven is heating up, grease a large muffin pan with cooking spray.
B. Then add the all-purpose flour, granulated sugar, baking powder, and soda to a large bowl. Stir well to mix.
C. Add the large egg and eggnog to a separate medium bowl. Stir well to mix. Add in the melted butter and stir well to incorporate.
D. Pour the eggnog mixture into the flour mixture. Stir well to mix.
E. Pour the batter into the greased muffin pan. Place into the oven to bake for 8 to 10 minutes or until baked through.
F. While the muffins are baking, prepare the glaze. To do this add the powdered sugar, rum, remaining eggnog, and cinnamon to a small bowl. Whisk well until smooth in consistency.
G. Remove the muffins from the oven. Allow it to cool for 10 minutes before dipping the muffins into the glaze. Transfer to a wire rack to cool completely.

4. Eggnog Tarts

Yield: 24 Servings

Cooking Time: 3 Hours

Ingredient List:

- 1 pack of vanilla pudding mix
- 1 envelope of unflavored gelatin
- ⅛ teaspoons of ground nutmeg
- 3 cups of store-bought eggnog
- ½ cup of heavy whipping cream, whipped
- 24 tart shells
- A dash of ground nutmeg, for garnish

ooooooooooooooooooooooooooooooooooooooooo

How to Cook:

A. First, bake the tart shells per the directions on the package.

B. While the tart shells are baking, place a medium saucepan over medium heat. Add in the vanilla pudding mix, unflavored gelatin, and a dash of ground nutmeg. Add in the eggnog and stir to mix. Cook for 5 minutes, or until the mixture comes to a boil.

C. Remove from the heat and set in the fridge to chill for 1 hour.

D. Then beat the pudding mixture in a medium bowl. Beat until fluffy in consistency. Add the whipped heavy whipping cream and fold to incorporate.

E. Spoon this mixture into the tart shells.

F. Place into the fridge to chill for 2 hours, or until set.

G. After this sprinkle a dash of nutmeg over the top and serve.

5. Blueberry and Egg Nog Stuffed French Toast

Yield: 6 Servings

Cooking Time: 25 Minutes

Ingredient List:

- 5 eggs, whole and large
- 1 ¼ cups of eggnog
- ½ teaspoons of ground cinnamon
- ½ teaspoons of ground nutmeg
- Dash of coconut oil
- 1 loaf of Texas toast, sliced into thick slices
- 8 ounces of cream cheese, soft
- 3 tablespoons of powdered sugar
- 1 pint of blueberries, fresh
- Powdered sugar, for garnish
- Syrup, for serving

OOOOOOOOOOOOOOOOOOOOOOOOOOOOOOOOOOOOOOOO

How to Cook:

A. Add the egg, eggnog, ground cinnamon, and ground nutmeg to a large bowl. Whisk well to mix and set aside.

B. Place a large griddle over medium to high heat. Add in the touch of coconut oil.

C. Dip the Texas toast slices into the eggnog mixture, making sure to coat on both sides.

D. Transfer the toast slices to the griddle. Cook for 3 to 5 minutes on each side or until golden. Remove and transfer to a plate. Repeat with the remaining Texas toast.

E. While the toast is cooking add the cream cheese and powdered sugar to a small bowl. Whisk until smooth in consistency.

F. Serve the bread slices with the cream cheese mixture spread over the top.

G. Top off with the blueberries, powdered sugar, and syrup.

6. Spiced Eggnog Bundt Cake

Yield: 8 Servings

Cooking Time: 1 Hour

Ingredient List for the cake:

- 1 cup of butter, soft
- 3 cups of granulated sugar
- 6 eggs, large
- 3 cups of cake flour
- ¾ teaspoons of baking powder
- ½ teaspoons of salt
- 1 cup of eggnog
- 2 teaspoons of pure vanilla
- 2 tablespoons of dark rum
- 1 teaspoon of ground cinnamon
- ¾ teaspoons of ground nutmeg
- ½ teaspoons of ground allspice
- ¼ teaspoons of ground cloves

Ingredient List for the glaze:

- 1 cup of powdered sugar
- 2 tablespoons + 1 teaspoon of heavy whipping cream

OOOOOOOOOOOOOOOOOOOOOOOOOOOOOOOOOOOOOOOO

How to Cook:

A. Begin by preheating the oven to 350°F. While the oven is heating up, grease a large Bundt cake pan and sprinkle a touch of flour over the top.

B. Add the butter to the bowl of a stand mixer. Beat for 2 minutes on the medium setting until creamy in consistency. Add in the granulated sugar and eggs. Continue to beat for 5 minutes or until creamy.

C. Add the all-purpose flour, baking powder, and dash of salt to a separate large bowl. Stir well to mix and add in the butter mixture. Add in the eggnog and stir well until just mixed. Add in the pure vanilla and stir again to incorporate.

D. Pour half of the batter into the greased Bundt pan.

E. Pour the ground cinnamon, ground nutmeg, ground allspice, and ground cloves into the remaining cake batter. Stir well to mix. Pour the remaining batter into the bundt pan.

F. Place into the oven to bake for 50 to 55 minutes, or until cooked Remove and set aside to cool for 15 minutes. Remove from the pan.

G. While the cake is cooling, prepare the glaze. To do this add the powdered sugar and heavy cream to a medium bowl. Whisk until smooth in consistency.

H. Pour the glaze over the cooled cake and serve.

7. Eggnog Cheesecake

Yield: 12 Servings

Cooking Time: 2 Hours and 10 Minutes

Ingredient List:

- 12 ounces of gingersnaps, ground
- ¼ cup of granulated sugar
- ¼ cup of melted butter
- 32 ounces of low-fat cream cheese
- 4 eggs, large
- 2 cups of eggnog, canned and divided
- 2 cups of powdered sugar
- 2 tablespoons of all-purpose flour
- 1 cup of heavy whipping cream
- Nutmeg, grated

OOOOOOOOOOOOOOOOOOOOOOOOOOOOOOOOOOOOOOO

How to Cook:

A. Add the ground gingersnaps, granulated sugar, and melted butter to a large bowl. Stir well until mixed and press this mixture into the bottom of a large springform pan.

B. Then add the cream cheese, eggs, 1 ½ cups of eggnog, powdered sugar, and all-purpose flour to a large bowl. Beat with an electric mixer until just mixed.

C. Pour the cream cheese mixture over the crust.

D. Place into the oven to bake at 325°F for 1 hour. Turn off the oven after this time and allow it to stand with the oven door open for an additional hour. After this time transfer to a wire rack to cool completely. Once cooled, cover and set into the fridge to chill for 8 hours.

E. While the cheesecake is chilling add the heavy whipping cream to a medium bowl. Beat with an electric mixer until peaks begin to form on the surface. Add in the remaining half a cup of eggnog and beat to incorporate.

F. Spread the cream mixture over the top of the cheesecake. Serve.

8. Eggnog Donuts

Yield: 8 to 10 Servings

Cooking Time: 20 Minutes

Ingredient List for the donuts:

- 2 cups of all-purpose flour
- ¾ cup of granulated sugar
- 1 teaspoon each of baker's style baking powder and soda
- 1 teaspoon of salt
- ½ teaspoons of nutmeg
- 1 egg, large
- ¾ cup of eggnog
- ¼ cup of applesauce

Ingredient List for the icing:

- 1 ½ cups of powdered sugar
- 3 tablespoons of eggnog
- 1 teaspoon of rum flavoring
- A dash of nutmeg

OOOOOOOOOOOOOOOOOOOOOOOOOOOOOOOOOOOOOOO

How to Cook:

A. Add the all-purpose flour, granulated sugar, baking soda and powder, dash of salt, and ground nutmeg to a large bowl.

B. Add in the egg, applesauce, and eggnog. Stir well to incorporate.

C. Grease a large donut pan.

D. Pour the donut batter into a large Ziploc bag. Cut the corner and pipe the batter carefully into the donut pan.

E. Place into the oven to bake for 10 to 12 minutes at 325°F, or until the donuts are cooked through.

F. Remove the donuts from the donut pan and set them aside on a wire rack to cool.

G. While the donuts are cooling, prepare the glaze. To do this add the powdered sugar, rum flavoring, and eggnog to a medium bowl. Beat with an electric mixer for 2 to 3 minutes, or until smooth in consistency.

H. Dip the tops of the donuts into the glaze. Sprinkle a dash of nutmeg over each donut and serve.

9. Spiced Eggnog Cake

Yield: 10 Servings

Cooking Time: 2 Hours and 25 Minutes

Ingredient List for the eggnog cake:

- 1 ½ cups of all-purpose flour
- 1 ½ teaspoons of baker's style baking powder
- ½ teaspoons each of salt and ground nutmeg
- ¼ teaspoons of ground cinnamon
- ½ cup of unsalted butter
- ½ cup of granulated sugar
- ½ cup of brown sugar, light and packed
- 2 eggs, large
- 1 teaspoon of pure vanilla
- ¾ cup of eggnog

Ingredient List for the rum syrup:

- ½ cup of water
- ½ cup of granulated sugar
- 1 tablespoon of rum

Ingredient List for the cream cheese frosting:

- 1 cup of unsalted butter
- 6 ounces of cream cheese
- 3 cups of powdered sugar
- 1 teaspoon of pure vanilla
- ½ teaspoons of ground nutmeg

Ingredient List for the ganache:

- 3 ounces of white chocolate, chopped
- 1 ounce of heavy whipping cream

oooooooooooooooooooooooooooooooooooooooooo

How to Cook:

A. Preheat the oven to 350°F. While the oven is heating up grease and flour, three large cake pans. Line the cake pans with sheets of parchment paper.

B. Add the all-purpose flour, baking powder, ground nutmeg, ground cinnamon and dash of salt to a medium bowl. Stir well to mix and set aside.

C. Add the butter, granulated sugar, and brown sugar to the bowl of a stand mixer. Beat with an electric mixer until fluffy in consistency.

D. Add the eggs and pure vanilla. Beat until evenly incorporated.

E. Add the flour mixture and eggnog to the wet mixture. Stir until just mixed.

F. Pour the batter into the cake pans.

G. Place into the oven to bake for 25 to 30 minutes, or until baked through. Remove and transfer the cakes to a wire rack to cool completely.

H. While the cake is cooling, place a small saucepan over high heat. Add in the sugar and water. Whisk until the sugar has dissolved. Remove from the heat and add the rum. Stir well to mix. Set aside to cool.

I. Add the butter, cream cheese, powdered sugar, pure vanilla, and nutmeg to a medium bowl. Beat with an electric mixer until fluffy in consistency.

J. Place the chopped chocolate and heavy cream into a bowl. Microwave for 30 seconds, or until melted. Stir well until smooth in consistency. Set aside to cool.

K. Place one layer of the cake onto a large serving plate. Top off with ⅔ of the frosting. Repeat with the remaining cake layers. Place together and place into the fridge to chill for 20 minutes.

L. Drizzle the chocolate ganache over the sides of the cake. Sprinkle a touch of nutmeg over the top and place back into the fridge to chill for 15 minutes. Serve.

10. Quick Eggnog Bread

Yield: 8 Servings

Cooking Time: 55 Minutes

Ingredient List:

- 2 eggs, large
- 1 cup of granulated sugar
- 1 cup of eggnog
- ½ cup of butter, melted
- 2 teaspoons of rum
- 1 teaspoon of pure vanilla
- 2 ¼ cups of all-purpose flour
- 2 teaspoons of baking powder
- ¼ teaspoons of nutmeg

Ingredient List for the glaze:

- ¾ cup of powdered sugar
- Eggnog, as needed

ooooooooooooooooooooooooooooooooooooooooo

How to Cook:

A. Use a large bowl to mix the eggs, granulated sugar, eggnog, melted butter, rum, and pure vanilla. Stir well until just mixed.
B. Pour the batter into a large loaf pan.
C. Place into the oven to bake at 350°F for 45 to 50 minutes.
D. Remove and transfer to a wire rack to cool.
E. Make the glaze. To do this add the powdered sugar to a small bowl. Drizzle as much eggnog as you need until a smooth glaze begins to form.
F. Pour the glaze over the bread. Allow to stand for 5 minutes or until the glaze is set. Serve.

11. Gingerbread and Eggnog Cream Bars

Yield: 16 Servings

Cooking Time: 30 Minutes

Ingredient List for the bars:

- ½ cup of butter, soft
- ½ cup of sugar
- ⅓ cup of brown sugar, light and packed
- 1 egg, large
- 1 teaspoon of pure vanilla
- 3 tablespoons of molasses
- 2 cups of all-purpose flour
- 1 teaspoon of baker's style baking soda
- 1 teaspoon of ground cinnamon
- ½ teaspoons of ginger
- ¼ teaspoons of nutmeg
- ¼ teaspoons of allspice
- ½ teaspoons of salt

Ingredient List for the frosting:

- 4 ounces of cream cheese, soft
- 2 tablespoons of butter, soft
- 1 ¼ cup of powdered sugar
- 1 tablespoon of eggnog
- Sprinkles, optional

OOOOOOOOOOOOOOOOOOOOOOOOOOOOOOOOOOOOOOO

How to Cook:

A. Preheat the oven to 350°F. While the oven is heating up, grease a large baking dish with cooking spray.

B. Add the butter, granulated sugar, and light brown sugar to the large bowl of a stand mixer. Beat with an electric mixer until creamy in consistency. Add in the large egg, pure vanilla, and molasses. Beat again to mix.

C. Add the all-purpose flour, ground cinnamon, nutmeg, allspice, a dash of salt, and baking soda to a separate bowl. Stir well to mix before adding to the butter mixture. Beat again until just mixed.

D. Pour the batter into the baking dish.

E. Place into the oven to bake for 20 to 25 minutes, or until the edges are golden brown. Remove and transfer to a wire rack to cool.

F. While the bars are cooling, prepare the frosting. To do this add the cream cheese, butter, powdered sugar, and eggnog to a small bowl. Beat with an electric mixer until smooth in consistency.

G. Spread the frosting over the bars. Sprinkle the sprinkles over the top.

H. Cut into bars and serve.

12. Eggnog Kringle

Yield: 40 Servings

Cooking Time: 1 Hour and 50 Minutes

Ingredient List:

- ¼ teaspoons of salt
- ¼ teaspoons of ground cardamom
- 1 egg
- ½ cup of butter, soft
- ¾ cup of granulated sugar
- 1 teaspoon each of baking powder and soda
- 1 teaspoon of nutmeg, grated
- ½ teaspoons of pure vanilla
- ½ teaspoons of rum extract
- 3 cups of all-purpose flour
- ¾ cup of eggnog
- A dash of nutmeg, grated

OOOOOOOOOOOOOOOOOOOOOOOOOOOOOOOOOOOOOOOO

How to Cook:

A. Add the butter to a large bowl. Beat with an electric mixer until creamy in consistency.

B. Add the granulated sugar, baking powder, baking soda, grated nutmeg, a dash of salt, a large egg, pure vanilla, and rum. Beat well until evenly mixed.

C. Add the all-purpose flour and eggnog. Stir well to mix.

D. Divide the dough in half and wrap each half in a sheet of plastic wrap. Place into the fridge to chill for 1 hour.

E. Then preheat the oven to 425°F.

F. On a lightly floured surface roll out each half of the dough into a 10 by 5 rectangle. Cut the rectangle crosswise into thin strips. Roll each of these strips into a rope and shape each rope into a loop, making sure to cross the rope over itself. Twist the rope where it crossed and place it onto a large baking sheet. Repeat with the remaining ropes.

G. Place into the oven to bake for 5 minutes or until light brown. Remove and place onto a wire rack to cool. Sprinkle a dash of grated nutmeg over the top and serve.

13. No Bake Eggnog Pie

Yield: 6 to 8 Servings

Cooking Time: 3 Hours and 10 Minutes

Ingredient List:

- 1, 3.4-ounce pack of instant vanilla pudding

- 2 cups of eggnog, cold

- 1 cup of whipped topping, thawed

- 1 graham cracker pie crust

- Whipped topping, for topping

- Ground nutmeg, for serving

OOOOOOOOOOOOOOOOOOOOOOOOOOOOOOOOOOOOOOOO

How to Cook:

A. Add the instant vanilla pudding mixture and eggnog to a large bowl. Beat with an electric mixer until creamy in consistency.
B. Add in one cup of the whipped topping and beat until evenly mixed.
C. Pour the mixture into the prepared pie crust.
D. Place into the fridge to chill for 2 to 3 hours.
E. Serve with a dollop of whipped topping and a sprinkling of ground nutmeg.

Yield: 14 Servings

Cooking Time: 40 Minutes

Ingredient List:

- 1 tablespoon of instant yeast
- ¼ cup of warm water
- ¼ cup of granulated sugar
- ½ teaspoons of salt
- ½ teaspoons of nutmeg
- 1 ¼ cups of eggnog
- ¼ cup of vegetable oil
- 3 to 3 ½ cups of all-purpose flour
- ½ cup of raisins

Ingredient List for the glaze:

- ¾ cup of powdered sugar
- 1 to 2 tablespoons of eggnog
- ¼ teaspoons of pure vanilla
- A dash of nutmeg, grated

OOOOOOOOOOOOOOOOOOOOOOOOOOOOOOOOOOOOOO

How to Cook:

A. Add the yeast and water to a small bowl. Whisk to dissolve and set aside for 5 minutes or until foamy.

B. Then use a large bowl to combine the all-purpose flour, granulated sugar, dash of salt, grated nutmeg, and vegetable oil. Stir well to mix.

C. Add the craisins and yeast mixture. Stir well until a dough begins to form.

D. Knead the dough on a greased surface until smooth.

E. Cover the dough with a sheet of plastic wrap and set aside to rest for 15 to 20 minutes. After this, divide the dough in half.

F. Divide each dough half into three pieces. Roll each piece into a long rope and braid the three ropes together, making sure to tuck the ends under the bread.

G. Place the dough onto a large cookie sheet and repeat with the remaining dough. Set aside to rise for 1 hour or until doubled in size.

H. After this place the dough into the oven to bake at 350°F for 20 to 25 minutes or until light brown. Remove and allow to cool.

I. While the bread is cooling, make the glaze. Add all the ingredients listed for the glaze to a small bowl. Whisk until smooth in consistency.

J. Drizzle the glaze over the bread and serve.

15. White Chocolate Chip Eggnog Cookies

Yield: 24 Servings

Cooking Time: 20 Minutes

Ingredient List:

- 1 teaspoon of nutmeg
- 2 ½ cups of all-purpose flour
- ½ teaspoons of salt
- ½ teaspoons each of baker's style baking soda and powder
- 2 teaspoons of ground cinnamon
- ½ cup of butter, soft
- ¾ cup of granulated sugar
- ½ cup of brown sugar, light and packed
- ½ cup of eggnog
- 1 egg
- 2 teaspoons of pure vanilla
- 1 cup of white chocolate chips

OOOOOOOOOOOOOOOOOOOOOOOOOOOOOOOOOOOOOOOO

How to Cook:

A. Add the all-purpose flour, dash of salt, baking soda and powder, ground cinnamon, and nutmeg to a large bowl. Stir well to mix.

B. Add the soft butter, light brown sugar, and granulated sugar to a separate bowl. Using an electric mixer, beat the mixture until it is creamy in consistency. Add the pure vanilla, a large egg, and eggnog. Continue to beat until smooth.

C. Add in the flour mixture and stir well until just mixed.

D. Add in the white chocolate chips and fold to incorporate.

E. Place the mixture into the fridge to chill for 24 hours.

F. After this time, preheat the oven to 350 °F.

G. Grease a large cookie sheet with cooking spray and divide the dough into small bowls. Place onto the cookie sheet.

H. Place into the oven to bake for 15 minutes, or until baked through. Remove and allow to cool for 5 minutes before serving.

16. Eggnog Fudge

Yield: 100 Servings

Cooking Time: 30 Minutes

Ingredient List:

- 2 cups of granulated sugar
- ½ cup of butter, cut into small pieces
- ¾ cup of eggnog
- 11 ounces of white chocolate chips
- 1, a 7-ounce jar of marshmallow crème
- 1 teaspoon of pure vanilla
- ¼ teaspoons of ground nutmeg

OOOOOOOOOOOOOOOOOOOOOOOOOOOOOOOOOOOOOOOO

How to Cook:

A. Line a large baking pan with a sheet of parchment paper.
B. Place a medium pot over medium to high heat. Add the granulated sugar, butter pieces, and eggnog. Stir to mix and allow the mixture to come to a boil. Once boiling, remove from the heat.
C. Add the white chocolate and stir well until the chocolate is melted.
D. Add in the marshmallow crème, pure vanilla, and ground nutmeg. Stir until smooth in consistency.
E. Pour the mixture into the prepared baking pan. Set aside to cool to room temperature.
F. After this time cut 10 by 10 rows in the fudge.
G. Transfer into the fridge to chill completely before serving.

17. Eggnog French Toast Casserole

Yield: 8 Servings

Cooking Time: 1 Hour and 25 Minutes

Ingredient List:

- ½ cup of silk almond eggnog
- 1 loaf of French bread, cut into cubes
- 3 eggs, large and beaten
- 2 tablespoons of brown sugar, light and packed
- ⅛ teaspoons of ground cinnamon
- A dash of nutmeg, grated
- A dash of sea salt
- ½ cup of almonds, thinly sliced

Ingredient List for the glaze:

- 1 ½ cups of powdered sugar
- ¼ cup of silk almond eggnog

OOOOOOOOOOOOOOOOOOOOOOOOOOOOOOOOOOOOOOO

How to Cook:

A. Add the almond eggnog, large eggs, light brown sugar, ground cinnamon, ground nutmeg, and a dash of salt. Stir well to mix.

B. Add the breadcrumbs, sliced almonds, and eggnog mixture to a separate large bowl. Toss well until the bread is coated.

C. Transfer the coated bread cubes into a large baking dish that has been greased.

D. Allow to sit for 1 hour.

E. Preheat the oven to 375°F.

F. Place the casserole into the oven to bake for 20 minutes. Remove and set aside to cool slightly.

G. While the casserole is baking, prepare the glaze. To do this add all the Ingredient List for the glaze into a small bowl. Whisk until smooth in consistency.

H. Drizzle the glaze over the casserole dish. Sprinkle a touch of powdered sugar, ground cinnamon, and nutmeg over the top. Serve.

18. Eggnog Cheesecake Trifle

Yield: 2 Servings

Cooking Time: 1 Hour and 10 Minutes

Ingredient List:

- 1, 16-ounce pack of gingersnap cookies, chopped
- 1, a 4-ounce box of vanilla pudding mix
- 1 ¼ cups of eggnog
- 1 ½ cups of whipping cream
- ⅓ cup of confectioner's sugar
- 1, 8-ounce pack of cream cheese, soft
- ½ teaspoons of rum extract
- ¼ teaspoons of ground nutmeg, extra for garnish
- 6 cups of raspberries, extra for garnish
- 10 gingerbread cookies

OOOOOOOOOOOOOOOOOOOOOOOOOOOOOOOOOOOOOOOO

How to Cook:

A. Place a large bowl into the freezer to chill for 10 to 20 minutes

B. Add the vanilla pudding and eggnog to a large bowl. Whisk until mixed.

C. Pour the whipping cream and confectioner's sugar into the chilled bowl. Beat with an electric mixer until peaks begin to form on the surface. Pour into a separate bowl and set into the fridge to chill.

D. Add the cream cheese to the same chilled bowl. Beat with an electric mixer until creamy in consistency. Add the pudding mix to the cream cheese and beat again. Add half of the whipped cream and stir to mix.

E. Add the rum extract and grated nutmeg. Fold gently to mix.

F. Take a large trifle bowl and in it, layer half of the chopped gingersnaps on the bottom. Scoop half of the eggnog mixture over the cookies. Repeat with the remaining cookies and eggnog mixture. Add the whipped cream mixture over the top.

G. Top off with raspberries and gingerbread cookies.

H. Place into the fridge to chill for 1 hour. Serve.

19. Eggnog Truffles

Yield: 24 Servings

Cooking Time: 3 Hours and 30 Minutes

Ingredient List:

- 2 cups of granulated sugar
- ¾ cup of eggnog
- ½ cup of butter, soft
- 1 teaspoon of rum flavoring
- 1 teaspoon of nutmeg
- 1 cup of marshmallow cream
- 3 cups of white chocolate morsels
- 2, 16-ounce packs of vanilla candy coating
- 1 tablespoon of nutmeg, for garnish

OOOOOOOOOOOOOOOOOOOOOOOOOOOOOOOOOOOOOOOO

How to Cook:

A. Add the granulated sugar, eggnog, and soft butter to a large pot. Set over medium heat and bring the mixture to a boil. Once it begins to boil, remove it from the heat and add the rum flavoring and nutmeg. Stir well to mix.

B. Transfer this mixture to a large bowl. Add in the marshmallow cream and white chocolate morsels. Stir well until the chocolate is melted.

C. Pour the chocolate mixture into a large baking sheet lined with a sheet of parchment paper. Place into the fridge to chill for 1 to 2 hours.

D. Cut the chocolate mixture into small pieces. Roll each of these pieces into a ball and place them back onto the baking sheet. Place into the freezer to chill for 1 hour.

E. Melt the vanilla candy coating and transfer to a large bowl.

F. Dip each of the truffles into the melted chocolate, making sure to shake off the excess. Place back onto the baking sheet.

G. Sprinkle a touch of nutmeg on the top of each truffle.

H. Place back into the fridge to chill for 30 minutes before serving.

20. Eggnog Custard

Yield: 8 Servings

Cooking Time: 2 Hours

Ingredient List:

- 1 refrigerated pie crust, soft
- ½ cup of granulated sugar
- 2 ½ cups of eggnog
- 3 eggs, large
- Dash of nutmeg, grated

OOOOOOOOOOOOOOOOOOOOOOOOOOOOOOOOOOOOOOOOO

How to Cook:

A. Preheat the oven to 425°F.
B. Place the pie crust onto a large baking sheet. Place into the oven to bake for 8 to 10 minutes, or until light brown. Remove and set aside.
C. Reduce the temperature in the oven to 350°F.
D. Add the granulated sugar, eggnog, and eggs to a large bowl. Stir well to mix.
E. Pour this mixture into the baked pie crust. Sprinkle the grated nutmeg over the top.
F. Place into the oven and cover with a sheet of aluminum foil. Bake for 35 minutes. After this time remove the aluminum foil and continue to bake for an additional 20 to 30 minutes.
G. Remove and transfer into the fridge to chill for 2 hours. Serve.

21. Classic Eggnog Lamingtons

Yield: 8 Servings

Cooking Time: 45 Minutes

Ingredient List:

- 1 cup of granulated sugar
- ½ cup of butter
- 3 eggs, large
- 2 cups of all-purpose flour
- 2 teaspoons of baking powder
- ½ teaspoons of salt
- 1 tablespoon of pure vanilla
- ½ cup of eggnog
- 3 to 4 cups of coconut, blended

Ingredient List for the icing:

- ¾ cup of white chocolate chips
- 3 tablespoons of butter
- ½ cup of eggnog
- 1 ½ cups of powdered sugar

OOOOOOOOOOOOOOOOOOOOOOOOOOOOOOOOOOOOOOOO

How to Cook:

A. Preheat the oven to 350°F. While the oven is heating up, grease a large baking dish and line it with a sheet of parchment paper.

B. Then add the butter, granulated sugar, and eggs to a large bowl. Beat with an electric mixer until mixed.

C. Add the all-purpose flour, baking powder, and dash of salt. Beat again until evenly blended.

D. Add in the pure vanilla and eggnog. Stir well until just mixed.

E. Pour the batter into the prepared pan. Place into the oven to bake for 30 minutes, or until golden. Remove and allow to cool in the pan and then transfer to a wire rack. Allow to completely cool.

F. Add the blended coconut to a medium bowl.

G. Then prepare the icing. To do this place a medium saucepan over medium heat. Add in the white chocolate chips, butter, and eggnog. Stir well to mix and cook for 1 to 2 minutes, or until melted. Remove from the heat and add the powdered sugar. Stir well until smooth in consistency.

H. Cut the baked cake into bars. Spoon the icing over the top and sprinkle the coconut over the icing.

22. Eggnog Cinnamon Rolls

Yield: 12 Servings

Cooking Time: 2 Hours and 45 Minutes

Ingredient List for the dough:

- 1 cup of eggnog, warm
- ⅔ cup of granulated sugar
- 1 ½ tablespoon of active dry yeast
- 1 stick of unsalted butter, soft
- 2 eggs, large
- ½ teaspoons of sea salt
- 4 ½ cups of unbleached white flour

Ingredient List for the filling:

- ¾ cup of brown sugar, light and packed
- 1 ½ tablespoon of ground cinnamon
- ½ cup of butter, soft

Ingredient List for the frosting:

- 1 cup of confectioner's sugar
- 3 tablespoons of butter, melted
- 2 ounces of cream cheese
- 1 ½ tablespoon of eggnog

OOOOOOOOOOOOOOOOOOOOOOOOOOOOOOOOOOOOOOOO

How to Cook:

A. Add the eggnog, granulated sugar, and yeast to the large bowl of a stand mixer. Beat with a dough hook until the yeast is foamy.
B. Add in the soft butter, large eggs, and a dash of sea salt. Continue to beat until mixed.
C. Add in the unbleached white flour and continue to beat until a soft dough begins to form.
D. Remove the dough from the bowl and place it onto a lightly greased surface. Knead the dough until it is smooth. Place into a greased bowl. Cover with a sheet of plastic wrap and then set aside to rest in a warm place for 1 ½ to 2 hours, or until doubled.
E. Line the bottom of a large baking dish with a sheet of parchment paper.
F. Place the dough onto a lightly greased surface and roll it into a large rectangle.
G. Meanwhile add the light brown sugar and ground cinnamon to a small bowl. Stir well to mix and sprinkle over the top of the dough.
H. Tightly roll the dough into a large log. Cut the log into small quarters and cut these pieces into four slices. Place the slices onto the large baking pan. Cover with a sheet of plastic wrap. Allow it to rise for 2 hours.
I. During this time, preheat the oven to 425°F.
J. Place the rolls into the oven to bake for 25 minutes, or until they are golden brown. Remove and transfer to a wire rack and let it cool for 30 minutes.
K. During this add the powdered sugar, butter, heavy cream, soft cream cheese, and eggnog to a small bowl. Beat until smooth in consistency.
L. Spread the frosting over the cooled cinnamon rolls. Serve immediately.

23. Eggnog Cake Mix Cookies

Yield: 8 Servings

Cooking Time: 12 Minutes

Ingredient List:

- 1 cup of yellow cake mix
- 3 tablespoons of unsalted butter, melted
- 1 egg yolk, large
- 1 tablespoon of cold eggnog
- ¼ teaspoons of ground nutmeg

Ingredient List for the frosting:

- ⅓ cup of powdered sugar
- 1 to 2 tablespoons of eggnog
- A dash of grated nutmeg, for garnish

OOOOOOOOOOOOOOOOOOOOOOOOOOOOOOOOOOOOOOOO

How to Cook:

A. Preheat the oven to 350°F.
B. While the oven is heating up, add all the ingredients to a small bowl. Stir well until just mixed.
C. Divide the dough into 8 small balls. Place onto a large baking sheet.
D. Place into the oven to bake for 10 minutes. Remove and allow to cool on a wire rack completely.
E. While the cookies are cooling, make the frosting. To do this add the powdered sugar and eggnog to a small bowl. Whisk until smooth in consistency.
F. Spread the frosting on each of the cookies.
G. Sprinkle the nutmeg over the top and serve.

24. Eggnog Mousse

Yield: 5 servings

Cooking Time: 40 Minutes

Ingredient List:

- 2 cups of ready-made eggnog
- 2 teaspoons of gelatin
- 1 ¼ cups of white chocolate
- ½ teaspoons of ground nutmeg
- 2 tablespoons of brandy
- 2 cups of heavy cream
- 2 teaspoons of pure vanilla

OOOOOOOOOOOOOOOOOOOOOOOOOOOOOOOOOOOOOOO

How to Cook:

A. Add the gelatin and the eggnog to a large saucepan set over medium heat. Cook for 5 minutes, or until it begins to bloom.
B. Reduce the heat to low and allow the gelatin to dissolve.
C. Remove from the heat and add the white chocolate and ground nutmeg. Whisk until smooth in
D. Allow to cool completely until the gelatin begins to set.
E. While the gelatin is cooling, add the heavy cream, pure vanilla, and brandy to a medium bowl. Beat with an electric mixer until peaks begin to form on the surface.
F. Fold the cream mixture into the eggnog mixture until just mixed.
G. Serve immediately.

25. No-Bake Eggnog Bites

Yield: 10 Servings

Cooking Time: 15 minutes

Ingredient List:

- 1 ¾ cups of gluten-free oat flour
- ¼ cup of coconut flour
- 1 scoop of protein powder, optional
- 2 tablespoons of granulated sweetener
- A dash of sea salt
- A dash of cloves
- A dash of ground nutmeg
- ¼ cup of cashew butter
- ¼ cup of brown rice syrup
- ¼ cup of silk eggnog
- Granulated sugar, for coating

OOOOOOOOOOOOOOOOOOOOOOOOOOOOOOOOOOOOOOO

How to Cook:

A. Add the oat flour, granulated sweetener, a dash of sea salt, and a dash of cloves to a large bowl. Stir well to mix.

B. Place a medium saucepan over medium heat. Add in the cashew butter. Once melted add in the granulated sweetener. Stir well to mix.

C. Pour the butter mixture into the flour mixture. Add in the silk eggnog and stir well until a thick batter begins to form.

D. Form the mixture into small balls. Roll each of these balls into the sugar mixture. Place onto a large baking sheet.

E. Place into the fridge to chill for 10 minutes, or until firm. Serve.

Author's Note

T H A N K   Y O U

Not many people do this, but I grew up under difficult circumstances where nothing was handed to me, and the only way forward was with your best effort. At some point, people started recognizing me for my talent in the kitchen despite my young age, and I've only worked harder from there!

Because I am constantly trying to improve my work, I would really appreciate your help. Sure, I always ask my friends and family for their feedback on my newest projects but, whether they want to accept it or not, there's always some sort of bias because they don't want to hurt my feelings by criticizing my work. Thus, I need a neutral pair of eyes — that's where you come in!

If you're up for it, I would appreciate you telling me what you think of my cookbooks. Are the recipes easy to follow? Did you get stuck somewhere? Are the measurements laid out? Any suggestions you may have are welcome. After all, cookbooks are only helpful when you actually understand them! Incorporating your ideas and suggestions into my new projects will be my show of eternal gratitude because you can only be the best at something by constantly improving and being open to change.

Thanks!

Alicia T. White

About the Author

Alicia had a tough childhood and had to take care of her siblings early. Although they often helped her with making the beds and washing, Alicia was responsible for cooking since she was the oldest of six. Being in the kitchen was still very difficult at her age, but she learned her way around the stove and oven throughout the years.

Whereas her first dishes were practically inedible, burnt rice and mushy pasta… Eventually, she turned to the oven for help as many of the dishes she wanted to make were too complicated. Nonetheless, her baked casseroles were amazing! Most importantly, they were simple and required way less clean-up.

At first, they were simple pasta bakes, but once Alicia got the hang of things, she was baking all sorts of meals. When it came to spreading the word of her delicious cooking, having 5 siblings was extremely advantageous. Soon, neighbors were placing orders for some of her casseroles! Eventually, Alicia was doing so well with the business that she hired extra help. Now it's one of the most affordable yet popular weeknight casserole services in the mid-West!

Today, she still lives with her siblings and is working hard to teach them about the family business that led them out of poverty. She likes to publish cookbooks on casseroles and one-pot meals in her free time— basically anything quick and easy. Her motto is, "If a seven-year-old can't make it, it isn't simple enough!"

www.ingramcontent.com/pod-product-compliance
Lightning Source LLC
Chambersburg PA
CBHW080848160726
47999CB00009B/3034